NOTRE HIGH SCHOOL, NORWICH

A CELEBRATION OF THE FIRST 150 YEARS
1864–2014

John Eady

SHIRE PUBLICATIONS

Published in Great Britain in 2014 by Shire Publications Ltd, PO Box 883, Oxford, OX1 9PL, UK.
PO Box 3985, New York, NY 10185-3985, USA.

E-mail: shire@shirebooks.co.uk   www.shirebooks.co.uk

© 2014 Shire Publications and Notre Dame High School, Norwich.

A CIP catalogue record for this book is available from the British Library.

ISBN-13: 978 0 74781 430 6

John Eady has asserted his right under the Copyright, Designs and Patents Act, 1988, to be identified as the author of this book.

Designed by Tony Truscott Designs, Sussex, UK and typeset in Perpetua and Gill Sans.
Editor Ruth Sheppard
Indexer Zoe Ross

Printed in China through Worldprint Ltd.

14 15 16 17 18   10 9 8 7 6 5 4 3 2 1

COVER IMAGE
Chapel windows and garden, 2011.

TITLE PAGE IMAGE
Pupils, 1934. Ruby Jolly, Mary Palmer, Biddy Armstrong, Ursula Denny, with Bernadette Henderson in the front.

CONTENTS PAGE IMAGE
Sponsored walk 2008. The sponsored walk is the school's main fundraising event for charitable causes. The current route goes round Whitlingham Broad.

ACKNOWLEDGEMENTS
I am grateful to many people without whose contributions this history would be incomplete. In particular, I am especially grateful to Jean Bunn SND, for her continuing enthusiasm and assiduous archiving of the school's records over many years; to Roy Money, who generously shared many recollections of his time here; and to his wife Sue, who thankfully saved many of the older photographs from being destroyed. I would like to thank Neil Cully, Jonathan Hooton and Celia Miller for awarding the commission, and Brian Conway for trusting me with the authorship. I am grateful to many staff for assistance with and contributions to the school photo archive, especially Graham Spratt and Alex Savage, and to ex-pupils and friends Angie Banham, Rosemary Turner, James Woodrow and Stephen Slack for their input. Editor Ruth Sheppard did an excellent job focusing my sprawling text.

Finally I must offer thanks for the support of my family, Denise, Alex, Izzy, Christy and Francisca, our Norwegian guest Maria and my assistant Jane Pagani, all of whom showed great patience with me during the gestation of this project.

IMAGE ACKNOWLEDGEMENTS
I am grateful to Steve Hunt at stevehuntphoto.org for permission to use one of his pictures as the cover of this book.

Other photographs are used courtesy of Norfolk County Council Library and Information Service Picture Norfolk archive, pages 8, 9, 10 (top), 14 (bottom), 41; Archant CM Ltd, Norfolk, pages 38, 57, 59 (top and middle), 60 (bottom); Bryn Colton/Assignments, page 52; Steve Hunt, pages 27 (bottom), 59 (bottom); Jane Palmer, page 43 (bottom); Jonathan Plunkett at the George Plunkett photo archive, pages 30 (bottom), 50 (bottom), and Stephen Slack, page 4. The pictures on pages 11 (top), 20 (top) and 22 (bottom) are taken from A Great Gothic Fane (W.T. Pike & Co., 1913).

All other photographs are from the archives of Notre Dame High School Norwich, or are in the public domain.

Shire Publications is supporting the Woodland Trust, the UK's leading woodland conservation charity, by funding the dedication of trees.

CONTENTS

PREFACE

It is an incredible privilege to be part of this wonderful school as it celebrates 150 years since its foundation by the Sisters of Notre Dame. I think that those six Sisters would be amazed by the changes that Notre Dame High School has seen in those 150 years – the buildings, the technology, the curriculum, even perhaps the presence of boys in this school. However, I think they would still recognise the core purpose and values that they embodied in their work. The founding Sisters of Notre Dame would see that our Catholic values inspire us and that we develop through caring for those around us. They would see that we know that a good education provides the best opportunity in life, and that we want everyone to be successful, to be happy, to feel loved and to feel part of a community. The Sisters would still recognise that the educational journey through Notre Dame, as we grow and develop, leaves a lasting impression and memories to treasure. I think their educational and spiritual values – placing our faith in God at the centre of what we do – still reverberates throughout this school and that ethos remains the powerful driving force behind this school.

This history of the first 150 years is a wonderful record of the work and achievements of the Sisters of Notre Dame, the many staff and the huge number of students who have passed through this school. On behalf of everyone currently involved with the school I would like to thank all who have been involved in the production of this book, and the legacy of all those who have contributed to the first 150 years of education at Notre Dame High School in Norwich.

Brian Conway
Head teacher

Opposite:
Cathedral Mass,
2010. The whole
school walk through
Norwich at the
beginning of the
school year to
celebrate Mass
at the Catholic
Cathedral on
Grapes Hill.

5

FIRST STEPS: NORWICH 1864

THE TRAIN FROM LONDON STEAMED SLOWLY IN TO Norwich station on the morning of 13 October 1864. Amongst the alighting passengers were six English Sisters of the Order of Notre Dame de Namur. The first nuns in Norwich since the Reformation, they were undoubtedly the object of much curiosity and some suspicion. First through the station barrier, carrying a statue of Our Lady, the Mother of Christ, was Sister Anne of St John. She was followed by Sister Stanislaus of the Immaculate Conception, Sister Aloyse of the Cross, Sister Clare of the Cross, the novice Sister Mary Anne Joseph and their Superior, Sister Mary of the Redemption. So began the story of the Sisters in Norwich, and the school they founded.

At that time, life in Norwich epitomised a mixture of Victorian practices and the foundations of modern society. For a city that was later proudly to boast it had a pub for every day of the year, in the mid-nineteenth century there were a staggering 600 pubs. Poverty was endemic, particularly in the notorious yards lining Ber Street, which housed deprived families in wretched conditions. The general health of the city population was extremely poor; in the 1870s medical journal *The Lancet* reported that Norwich had the highest mortality rate of twenty large towns and cities it had surveyed. The world the Sisters entered was undoubtedly harsh and brutal, with the last public hanging, from gallows erected between the gatehouses leading up to Norwich Castle, occurring as late as 1867. Nevertheless the city was the perfect place for the Sisters, whose mission to serve the poor and educate children concentrated on areas of urban deprivation, particularly in regions where there was a dearth of Catholics.

The Order of the Sisters of Notre Dame de Namur owed its existence to the founding vision of Julie Billiart, a villager from Cuvilly in Picardy, approximately 60 miles north of Paris. Born on 12 July 1751, Julie attended her village school, where her spirituality and gifts for communicating the love of God were soon recognised.

Opposite:
Saint Julie Billiart (1751–1816). Contemporary portrait of the founder of the Order.

Ber Street, 1908. The main thoroughfare for driving cattle to the huge market below the castle until 1960. Colloquially known as 'Blood and Guts' Street due to its association with the well-known butchery trade, Ber Street bordered the convent land and housed poor families in the squalid conditions of the yards. When the Sisters first arrived there were upwards of 25 pubs along this old Roman road.

The course of Julie's life was changed forever when she was twenty-three, for she was witness to an unsuccessful attempt on her father's life. This event precipitated a nervous condition in Julie, which was treated by blood letting. As a result, her legs became paralysed and she was bedridden, a condition she endured for the next twenty-two years. In spite of this affliction, Julie's gifts as a storyteller and teacher meant that people continued to flock to her bedside to receive teaching about God's goodness.

France in the late eighteenth century was a dangerous place, for the country was in the turmoil of the French Revolution. The established order of State and Church was under threat, and Julie, as a prominent and well-known Catholic, was in grave danger. With help, in 1790 she fled her village and went into hiding nearby. Whilst in hiding Julie had a vision of a group of women standing below Jesus' cross with the promise of the words 'Behold these spiritual daughters whom I give you in an Institute marked by the Cross'. She determined to follow her calling to found an order of nuns as God had instructed her to do.

Julie eventually took up lodgings in Amiens in 1794, staying in the home of the aristocratic Blin de Bourdon family. The daughter, Françoise, had been imprisoned and escaped the guillotine only by the fall of Robespierre, architect of the Reign of Terror. The two women struck up an unlikely friendship, based on their shared devotion to God.

On 2 February 1804 Julie and Françoise consecrated themselves to God 'in the person of the poor ones of Jesus Christ' and pledged themselves to the training of teachers specifically for the poor. This Mass marked the foundation of

Above: Globe Yard, Heigham Street, about 1916. Women and children dressed in their best clothes for this photo during the First World War.

Left: Bignold Yard, Surrey Street, 1930s. A typical scene from the yards, which were entered via passageways from the road.

Norwich
Station, 1863. A
contemporary
drawing.

Norwich
Station, 2014.

the Order of the Sisters of Notre Dame. Education and the training of
teachers were key aspects of the Order. Julie's faith shaped the core values,
whilst Françoise's fortune funded the purchase of property. Julie was
adamant that the Order should exist only for the poor, writing in 1808: 'I

ask you again to receive only poor little girls who cannot pay at all. Collect as many of them as you can. We exist only for the poor, only for the poor, absolutely only for the poor.'

The Sisters themselves took vows of poverty and lived an austere lifestyle, taking joy in the good God and in their service to others. '*Ah, qu'il est bon, le bon Dieu*' was Julie's most famous phrase, and became the motto of the Order – 'Ah, how good is the good God!'

Julie and Françoise moved to Namur (in present-day Belgium) where they established the Mother House of the Sisters of Notre Dame. Early missions to the United States (1844) and Britain (1845) were followed by spread of the Order worldwide. Today the Sisters represent the Order on five continents, and many thousands of children have benefited from their teaching.

On that October day in 1864, the six Sisters were met at Norwich station by Father John Dalton, canon of St John's Catholic chapel near Maddermarket. The canon gave over his own house, the run-down Strangers' Hall in the centre of the medieval city, until a suitable property could be secured for the Sisters. It seems a little ironic that this abode should be their first lodgings in Norwich, for it is named after Dutch and Flemish weavers who escaped Catholic persecution in Europe by travelling to East Anglia where they helped establish a very successful textiles trade.

Father John Dalton, who welcomed the Sisters at Norwich station.

The Sisters made a typical start for the Order – after Mass the following morning they set about cleaning the tumbledown building, several rooms of which were uninhabitable. On washing the floor in the main room, they were alarmed to hear cries from below – lodgers in the cellar protesting about the dirty water pouring through their ceiling!

At that time, Norwich was part of the vast Diocese of Northampton, which covered Bedford, Buckingham and Northampton as well as all of East Anglia. The bishop paid the Sisters a visit two days later, and on Monday 17 October they began their first teaching: at the school attached to St John's chapel near Maddermarket, and at the Jesuit school in Ten Bell Lane, off St Benedict's Street.

The crest of Notre Dame. The shield represents protection and faith, the stars the Blessed Trinity, the Cross the Resurrection, the crown eternal life and the fleur de lys the Blessed Virgin Mary. Saint Julie's motto translates as 'Ah, how good is the good God!'

THE HOUSE ON ST CATHERINE'S HILL

A NYONE WHO HAS STRUGGLED UP SURREY STREET at the tail end of an autumn term will know that it is one of the windiest streets in Norwich. This is due to its northwest–southeast orientation, its broad aspect lined with large buildings, and because it lies on a raised plateau which falls steeply away to the River Wensum on its eastern (Ber Street) side.

The school is situated on St Catherine's Hill, the southernmost triangle of land between Surrey Street and Ber Street, bounded by Chapel Loke and the Norwich Union (Aviva) buildings nearer the city centre. The area is named after St Catherine's church, whose grounds occupied the grassy area now bordering the inner ring road. This parish was decimated by the Black Death in 1348 and the church fell into disrepair, eventually to be pulled down.

Less than a year after their arrival in Norwich, the Sisters of Notre Dame de Namur bought the fine Georgian residence which at that time dominated St Catherine's Hill. In the same manner that Julie's vision had inspired the aristocrat Françoise Blin de Bourdon, the expansion of the Order in Britain was supported by the wealth of another heiress, Laura Stafford-Jerningham, who joined the Order and took the name Sister Mary of St Francis.

Laura Stafford-Jerningham, a local girl, was born at the magnificent Costessey Hall in 1811, the ninth of twelve children of Lord and Lady Stafford. She truly was the 'daughter of a hundred earls', for both sides of her family had proud aristocratic lineages. Just a few miles from Norwich, Costessey Hall was part of the property and land granted to Laura's ancestor Sir Henry Jerningham by Queen Mary I, as a reward for his support during her reign (1553–58).

A bright and sunny child, fluent in both French and Italian by the time she was seven, Laura had a happy and loving childhood. She showed an uncommon gift for judgement and diplomacy, gleaned in part from dinner party conversations with government ministers and other important persons visiting her parents.

Opposite:
The convent, 1905.

Laura Stafford-Jerningham (1811–86) as a young girl. For many years this portrait used to hang in the convent buildings, but its current whereabouts are unknown.

Below left: Costessey Hall showing the original Tudor Hall and large Catholic chapel built in the nineteenth century. After centuries in the Stafford-Jerningham family the Hall was finally lost early in the twentieth century when their lineage produced no heir. During the First World War the Hall was commandeered by the army and subsequently fell into disrepair; all that remains today is the ruined bell tower on the eighteenth fairway of Costessey Park golf club.

Below right: Costessey Hall drawing room, late nineteenth century.

In 1829 Laura married the Honourable Edward Petre, nephew of the Duke of Norfolk; he was thirty-five, she was eighteen. Laura accepted her parents' match for her and they had a happy life together, travelling extensively throughout Europe supporting Catholic charities. Laura quickly realised that in spite of her husband's wealth, he had no aptitude for business management. She took on the responsibility of running their combined estates, and rapidly proved herself a discerning and able financial and estates manager.

In 1848, following a short illness, Edward Petre died. Laura was thirty-seven, widowed and childless. She had always been attracted to the religious life, and soon after her husband's death she went to stay in Clapham, south London, at the small convent rented by the Sisters of Notre Dame. Her arrival was initially greeted with suspicion: why would a widowed aristocrat want to join the Order? But the Sisters soon recognised Laura's sincerity and integrity, and accepted her as a novice in their community.

It would have been a very different lifestyle for Laura, for at this time the Sisters slept in dormitories containing three or four curtained-off beds; it was only later that they had private 'cells'. Both dormitories and cells were austere, with no carpets and only a simple iron bedstead, a chair, a wardrobe, a small washstand and a writing table. Such basics remained the standard for the Order; the Sisters' cells in Norwich were similarly spartan, even when the convent closed one hundred and thirty years later. It was a lifestyle that spurned materialism, allowing the Sisters to focus on their relationship with the Divine and the education of the poor.

Laura took to the disciplines of the Order of Notre Dame immediately, and entered the Mother House in Namur in 1850, taking the name Sister Mary of St Francis. She turned over her inheritance to the Order, an act of exceptional generosity and selflessness.

Before Laura entered the Order its property in England amounted to just one rented convent, and the Superior General had been considering

withdrawing the Sisters back to the continent. Instead, Laura's endowment and business skills facilitated a huge expansion of the Order – when she died in 1886 the Sisters owned over twenty convents in Britain, the majority of which had been bought or built with her fortune. These included Norwich, Clapham, St George's (Southwark), St Helens, Blackburn, Sheffield, Plymouth, Northampton, Battersea, Birkdale, Wigan, Everton Valley and Mount Pleasant (Liverpool). Many of these have either schools or teacher training colleges attached.

It must have been particularly gratifying for Sister Mary of St Francis to purchase the house and grounds in Norwich, 6 miles from her childhood home. She visited the convent in 1867 and in 1872, and a picture of her in the Sisters' habit still hangs on the walls of St Julie's. Without her generosity and support of Catholic education Notre Dame High School would never have existed.

Sister Mary of St Francis wearing the heavy habit characteristic of the Order. In her hands she holds a rosary and a copy of the Bible. Along with the crucifix and table these amounted to the total possessions of individual Sisters in the early days.

Frustratingly, there seems to be no record of the original builder of the house on St Catherine's Hill, but it is contemporary with the work of celebrated Norwich architect Thomas Ivory, who was responsible for many of the Georgian buildings in and around Surrey Street. The house is first clearly shown on the 1789 Norwich map by Anthony Hochstetter, with the current demarcation of the grounds already in place.

The owner of the house was a Captain Ferdinand Ives. He had been educated at Harrow and Cambridge and had joined the army, rising to the level of captain before becoming a Justice of the Peace (magistrate) and the Deputy Lieutenant of Norfolk. He had a small household of six servants – a butler, a cook, a laundry maid, a housemaid, a footman and a groom; indeed the original stables are largely unchanged on the exterior, and are now used as a classroom adjoining the courtyard (which itself was once an enclosed quiet area for the Sisters).

Captain Ives enjoyed socialising and gambling, as befitted his standing in society, and hosted parties in what became the parlour of the convent (now the head teacher's office). However, over time the accumulation of gambling debts necessitated the sale of the house. What was the captain's loss became the Sisters' gain. On 16 June 1865 the community left their 'dear old ruins' (as they called their first home) to move into their new convent, which they were to refer to affectionately as 'Noah's Ark', a Biblical reference to its size and prominence.

The house was a convent for the Order for a hundred and thirty years, semi-closed to outsiders, although classes for children were housed there in both the early and final days. The grounds extended as far as Finkelgate, and have not altered much during the past century and a half, save for the

The House on St
Catherine's Hill,
about 1977.

Below: Corridor
in St Julie's. Taken
in 1994, when the
Sisters left the
convent, this picture
conveys the stately
elegance of the
Georgian interior.

Below left: In 1979
the main chapel was
used as a Christian
Education Centre,
and, from 1994 until
its re-dedication in
2004, as a drama
studio. In the
meantime one of
the rooms in the
convent was used as
a chapel. This is now
the school's pastoral
office.

Below right: Staff
room, St Julie's
1994. The elegant
bay-fronted room
as it was left by the
Sisters.

creation of the Lady Julian building in 1900 and the acquisition and
construction of St Peter's science facilities in 1979 and 2011. To the front, the
gardens ran down as far as the 1926 St John's building, with an orchard of
apple, pear and occasional plum trees bordering
the limits of the land. Immediately beyond,
Butcher's Alley ran from the present middle gate
on Surrey Street, parallel to where St John's now
stands, and up the slope by the fenced all-weather
surface, finally to emerge on Ber Street among
the yards near the site of the Jolly Butchers pub.
This alley remained a public thoroughfare and
shortcut between Surrey and Ber Streets until the
early twentieth century when the Order acquired
the land and the rights of passage.

The courtyard. Situated next to the house the buildings were originally stables, and the structure of the stable doors is still visible. Now an open route between St Julie's and the Sports Hall, the courtyard at one time was a quiet enclosed area for the Sisters.

Greenhouses were erected close to the convent, near where the chapel would be built, and there were gardens and a mixed orchard in the grounds towards the site of the St John's building. Further allotments were created near the St Catherine's building and where the fenced all-weather surface would later be built. With the help of the gardeners and caretakers the site was largely self-sufficient in fruit and vegetables, and the Sisters had little call on local traders. Instead they lived lives of austerity and some hardship, with minimal interest in material possessions or worldly wealth.

The convent garden. Backing onto the house the garden has hosted First Holy Communion groups and is now used as an area for Year 11 pupils.

THE EARLY SCHOOLS

THE STORY OF THE SCHOOL IS ONE OF GRADUAL CHANGE, framed by the acquisition of new property and the shifting uses of premises; at one time or another it has been a girls' day school, a girls' boarding school, a mixed preparatory school, a girls' direct grant grammar school, a mixed comprehensive and in its present status, a mixed academy.

The Sisters took their first classes at St John's chapel school (close by but separate to the Anglican St John's Maddermarket church), and at the Jesuit school in Ten Bell Lane, both of which had been established several years previously. The schools were poorly attended when the Sisters first arrived, with only six infants and eight junior-age children (and one set of slates!) at St John's, and twenty-five children at Ten Bell Lane. Numbers grew quickly and by the end of summer term 1865 there were 172 children attending the two schools.

In January 1865 the Sisters also opened a separate day school at St John's with about twenty pupils. This modest beginning marks the founding of the current school.

In June the Sisters moved to St Catherine's Hill where they were able to take boarders, while continuing their main work for the poor. Many Notre Dame convents in Britain ran both boarding schools and day schools, the income from the former helping fund the latter. For several years the Sisters taught both at their day school in the convent and at St John's chapel and other schools in the city, amongst them the Jesuit school in Willow Lane off St Giles.

The boarding school opened with nine girls, three from Norwich, three from London, one from Lancashire, a three-year-old from Ireland, and a child from India. This mix of children typified the make-up of the boarding school, which always drew the majority of its pupils from England, but also housed girls from Ireland, Europe and all around the world. Ages ranged from three up to nineteen, and the time spent as a pupil varied from a few weeks to several years. The curriculum focused on religious education but also included

Opposite:
Group of girls, 1911.
M. Eckersley,
M. Jenks, R. Jukes,
V. Roberts.

19

St John's Catholic chapel, Maddermarket, about 1880. The original site of the Sisters' first teaching on their arrival in Norwich, the premises now form part of the Maddermarket Theatre.

The entrance hall. From a postcard around 1900, this area is still used as main reception.

The Little Ones' classroom. The 'Little Ones' were the youngest pupils in the boarding school, some as young as three, who were taught in the convent. This elegant room was the parlour of the original house and has been the head teacher's office for many years. It has a fine marble fireplace and walls adorned with superb decorative plasterwork.

history, literature, science, geography, needlework and domestic economy. Grouping for lessons was based on aptitude rather than age.

In 1869 the former stables were extended to enable the day school to exist separately from the convent, in the current St Catherine's building. The Duke of Norfolk was concerned for the safety of the Sisters so close to the city, and funded a caretaker's lodge at the entrance to the convent site to provide some security. Further expansion to the convent added a new wing in 1883 with classrooms for the boarders, piano rooms, a new washhouse, kitchen and refectory, and a community room (called the 'Sainte Famille').

The schools grew modestly, celebrating the festivals of the Catholic year. Sixty days after Easter the boarders took part in the huge Corpus Christi processions at Costessey Hall to celebrate the Real Presence of

The boarding school hall. Taken soon after the construction of the Lady Julian building in 1900, part of the ground floor was originally used as a sports hall for the children.

Dining room, about 1905. The boarders' dining room on the ground floor of the Lady Julian building had an immaculately polished floor. Now used as the science 'classroom of the future' and its preparation room, the original space has been divided by a partition wall.

Above: A Sister and two girls, about 1900.

Above right: Pupil Kathleen Wheldon, about 1910.

Below: The grotto, 1896. A remarkable reconstruction of the site of St Bernadette's vision at Lourdes, the grotto was constructed close to the chapel, but sadly nothing of it remains today.

Christ in the Eucharist. The children wore white veils and dresses and took tea on the lawn, much to the bemusement of the Sisters. One later was to recall 'You lose yourself and then you go to half a dozen butlers all in a row. They bow to you and assure you that they don't know the whereabouts of your Sisters any more than you do'.

Despite setbacks such as the Norwich smallpox epidemic in 1872 (which sadly resulted in reduced numbers at the school), perhaps the major threat to the school in these early years was a proposal to construct the parish church of St John's on the convent land (just where the St John's High School building was later constructed). Plans were drawn up for this ambitious project, but the school was saved from development when the former Norwich jail site became available at the top of Grapes Hill. The Catholic Duke of Norfolk funded the construction, and building of the mighty parish church commenced in 1884, to be completed in 1910. When the Diocese of East Anglia came into being in 1976, the church became the second largest Catholic cathedral in England.

By 1882 there were twenty-nine girls at the boarding school and thirty-nine girls in the day school, the forerunner of the high school. Increasing numbers meant that at Easter 1890 a class of nine younger girls was formed from those attending the day school, a predecessor of the preparatory school that opened around the turn of the century. Older girls were set in classes in a middle school, but by 1893 it was realised

The Avenue. Taken from the Surrey Street entrance in 1905 this photo shows the sweep of the drive up to the convent building. The original plan of the paths is still in place.

Boarders and Sport the dog, 1905–06. Back row: M. Minns, J. Kavanaugh, B. Gosling, O. Tennant, P. Furniss, A. Gouvernant, W. Hasler, N. Gosling, A. Kavanaugh, M. Redmond; middle row: I. Tennant, T. Brawne, U. Challis, R. Eversley, M. Galpin, M. Sheppard, G. Groeven, I. Groeven, M. Rix; front row: V. Roberts, G. Roberts, E. Coghlan, F. Pamplin, M. de Paira, I. Riley, M. Rix, R. Lebrun.

that they would be better organised into a high school. The few newly admitted younger boys had lessons in separate classrooms.

The girls wore a uniform of blue cotton dresses, the colour most strongly associated with the Virgin Mary. The school placed a particular emphasis on feasts and activities related to Our Lady, including a remarkable recreation of the grotto in Lourdes in 1885, following Canon Duckett's return from the site of Saint Bernadette's vision in the French Pyrenees.

Tennis court on Lady Julian Green, 1910. The girls played tennis, hockey, lacrosse and cricket in the summer months.

The school continued to expand, and in order to accommodate increasing numbers a grand new wing for the boarding school (the current Lady Julian building) was opened at Easter 1900, with a *salle* (hall), a refectory, boarders' bonnet rooms (cloakrooms for their hats and coats) and airy dormitories above. Over a century later the building still looks notably modern, with high-ceilinged rooms and clean-cut lines, though these have at times been obscured by the rampant growth of ivy on the outside walls.

The schools continued to prosper during the early part of the twentieth century. In common with many of the other Notre Dame convents that

Girls' hockey, about 1910. Back row: S. Baines, M. Banham, K. Farrow; front row: K. Baines, D. Roskell, E. Baines.

Girls playing, about 1910.

Below left: Central Hall. A temporary building constructed on land acquired in 1915, 'Asbestos Hall' was rendered redundant by the construction of the immediately adjacent St John's Hall. It was removed in 1927.

Below: School uniform. A selection of uniforms over the years.

hosted both day pupils and boarders, the groups were largely taught separately and not encouraged to fraternise, for some parents of boarders objected to their daughters mixing with those of a lower social status.

Sadly the school caretaker was called up and killed in action during the First World War, but otherwise the convent was little affected by the conflict.

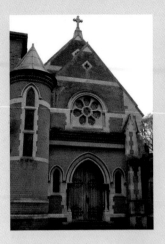

The chapel. Built in 1895–6 the mock-Gothic chapel remains central to the spiritual life of the school community.

Fleur-de-lys and cross mosaics on the floor supporting the altar. The fleur-de-lys is a symbol of Our Lady, the Mother of Christ.

Alabaster statues of the Blessed Virgin Mary holding the Gospel, and St John the Evangelist on the chapel altar.

THE GEM OF THE DIOCESE

In 1895 the Order granted the funds for a chapel to be constructed adjoining the convent in Norwich. The foundation stone was laid by Canon Duckett on 11 October and the chapel was finished in 1896. It was opened at the beginning of the autumn term by the bishop of Northampton.

In 1904 a new marble and alabaster altar was put up, with communion rails in brass and marble, and the following year an electric organ was installed. It is interesting to speculate that the marble – of which there are seven types – came from a small sample of the Italian and Greek marbles used to decorate the magnificent and contemporary Marble Hall of Norwich Union also in Surrey Street. This marble had originally been destined for Westminster Catholic cathedral, so it would be apt if a small portion of it had ended up in the chapel at Notre Dame.

The alabaster altar statues are of the Blessed Virgin Mary, St John the Evangelist, St Peter and St Mary Magdalene whilst the floor beneath has mosaics of fleurs-de-lys and crosses. The chapel is exquisitely beautiful, a rare example of a Victorian Catholic chapel.

Though it is a sanctuary of peace and tranquillity, the chapel has also been the site of dramatic events. The annals contain the following entry for 26 July 1911:

> The Prize Day. A great thunderstorm took place and our beautiful little chapel was struck. The fire brigade was at once summoned, and worked hard, but nothing could save the roof which was of pitch-pine, and it all fell in. The Sanctuary and High Altar was spared, and the walls also were intact, but the organ was spoilt. Happily the chapel and the organ were insured, but not the furniture. Desperate efforts were made by the Sisters, and all the benches, Stations of the Cross and statues were saved, as well as everything in the sacristies. When the priests arrived for the ceremony of the Distribution of Prizes, they gave what help they could. Thank God no-one was hurt, and after the priests had had dinner, the Prizes were given as arranged. It was a never-to-be-forgotten day.

The chapel is at the heart of the convent and the life of the school. Over the years it has hosted many First Communions,

The chapel interior. The altar canopy is adorned with five-pointed stars (symbolising the Epiphany) on a blue background above which is the text of the Gregorian chant '*Adoremus in Aeternum Sanctissimum Sacramentum*' (Let us adore for all eternity the Most Blessed Sacrament). The chapel was redecorated in 1937 when the canopy was painted: originally the wooden boards were unpainted.

Above: Chapel window from the inside.

Confirmations and Masses celebrated by visiting bishops and priests, and has remained a special place. Today it is used for Masses, and hosts events related to Mental Health Week, Refugee Week, bereavement groups and other pastoral support activities. It is always open for pupils and staff.

Bishop Frederick Keating (Bishop of Northampton 1908–21) was so struck by the beauty of the Norwich chapel that he called it 'the gem of the Diocese'. He was not wrong. It seems astonishing that the 1954 listing of Notre Dame as a Grade II building concentrates on the fine entrance porch to the convent, but notes that the 'Chapel adjoining to [the] right is not of special architectural interest.' One can only assume that the inspectors were not granted access.

Right: Tabernacle on the altar, used for storing the consecrated Eucharist prior to Holy Communion.

1926: THE GIRLS' HIGH SCHOOL

A HOUSE, AND LAND ADJOINING the convent orchard gardens, were purchased in 1915 to ease the crowding of the convent site. The building was called St Joseph's House and along with the temporary Central Hall, disturbingly referred to as 'Asbestos Hall', it was to house the high school pupils, who numbered 112 in 1916 but rose to 200 soon after the end of the First World War.

Towards the end of each summer term the Sisters rewarded the children by taking them on day trips to the seaside at Mundesley, Happisburgh, Yarmouth and Sea Palling, or occasionally to locations such as Walsingham. This was a chance for the children to relax and have fun, but the Sisters were still required to wear their full habit, even during the hottest days of summer. In the 1920s these trips seemed to epitomise the spirit of post-war optimism, and were greatly enjoyed by the pupils. The school record for 1927 reads 'July 4th. Sister Superior kindly gave the Preparatory School their annual picnic to Sea Palling. A gloriously happy day. Char-a-bancs started from school punctually at 10am and returned at 7pm....July 8th. Secondary school picnic to Sea Palling. Lovely day, no mishaps, great happiness for Sisters and children.'

The Sisters soon recognised that increasing numbers of girls at the day school meant that St Joseph's House and the adjoining Central Hall were not a long-term solution. Accordingly, they made plans for a more suitable building. Construction commenced in 1925, and the new high school was opened on 16 September 1926 to 238 day pupils, once the rooms (and the boilers!) had been blessed. The building was purchased partly out of funds provided by the second great benefactor of the Order in England, Sister Marie des Saints Anges (Mary Towneley).

The new school – St John's building – was equipped with a gymnasium (now used as art rooms), a science laboratory, cookery room, domestic science rooms, art and craft rooms, a library, a Lady chapel (now used as a small teaching room) and twelve classrooms overlooking the garden

Opposite: Head Girl and Heads of Houses, 1935. Left to right: M. Kirby (Head Girl), F. Butcher, L. Mitchell and A. Harrold in front of the playground wall with Surrey Street Elementary Schools beyond. These were acquired in the mid-1950s and one was used as the original St Mary's building.

Annual school
outing to Mundesley,
1935. Sister
Catherine of St
Joan, Sister St John,
Sister Cécile des
Seraphims and Sister
Mary Imelda on the
beach.

St Joseph's House,
1989. Bought in
1915 the building
housed high school
pupils and the
preparatory school,
and afterwards
Sixth Form pupils
and the geography
department. It was
sold in 1997.

Opposite: Girls
exiting St John's,
1935. The main
building of the
school from 1926.
The girls are walking
round the orchard
and all wear the
obligatory Panama
hat, which was not
to be removed
when outdoors,
even on the journey
to school!

and orchard. The assembly hall seated 400. This is the building that former pupils associate most strongly with the school, and the green tiles on every polished corridor, stairwell and classroom will undoubtedly be remembered by pupils for years to come.

Mundesley school trip, 1935.

St Joseph's House was effectively put into temporary storage for a number of years, and the old Central Hall was sold to the Ladies of Mary convent at Norwood. It was removed in May 1927, leaving a large playground area for the children.

A formal request for state recognition was made to the Ministry of Education in 1927, and following a rigorous inspection of physical training, science, geography, maths, Latin, English, French, history, needlework and religious education (RE) the school became a state-aided direct grant girls' grammar school, receiving funding from the government in exchange for offering some 'free' places. These girls were selected following their success

St John's with
crocuses, March
2009.

Opposite:
School report of
Eileen Harrison,
Preparatory Class 4,
spring term 1928.

at an entrance examination, taken in two stages. The majority of the pupils were from fee-paying families.

The boarding school was amalgamated with the high school in September 1927 so that lessons were shared, though the few residential pupils continued to use their own wing of the boarding school outside school hours. All 165 secondary school girls had their lessons on the second floor of St John's, whilst all 123 boys and girls in the preparatory classes were taught on the first floor. The students were organised into four Houses; Towneley and Stafford (recognising the two great benefactors of the school) and Walsingham and Lourdes (recognising sites of pilgrimage of Our Lady). Possibly because of organisational difficulties, one house, Lourdes, was dropped so that only three remained.

In 1930 the annals record the first occurrence of so-called 'Black Baby Day', a bazaar held in aid of foreign missionaries, followed by tea and a dance, which was very well attended. This became an annual event and large amounts of money were raised for the missions.

Also recorded are the dreaded 'semi-circles' held at the end of every term, when the Sister Superior of the convent (a position more senior than that of the Headmistress) came down to the assembly hall for the reading of the term's marks. Each form was called out in turn and their individual results were read to the whole school, from best to worst. Those achieving

A.M.D.G.

NOTRE DAME HIGH SCHOOL,

NORWICH.

ss *Eileen Harrison* _____ Attendance *Absent 5 times out of 116*

port for Term ending *4ᵗʰ April 1928* Form *Preparatory 4.*

duct *Very Good* Diligence *Very Good* Neatness *Very Good*

nctuality *Excellent* _____ Homework *Very Good*

Classification for these points: EXCELLENT, VERY GOOD, FAIRLY GOOD, UNSATISFACTORY.

entions _____

Marks obtained in School Examinations.

	Per cent.		Per cent.
LIGIOUS KNOWLEDGE :		**MATHEMATICS :**	
CHRISTIAN DOCTRINE	86	ARITHMETIC	52
OLD TESTAMENT ⎫	75	ALGEBRA	
NEW TESTAMENT ⎬		GEOMETRY	
CHURCH HISTORY			
		SCIENCE :	47
GLISH :	65	BOTANY	
GRAMMAR		DOMESTIC	
DICTATION	69		
COMPOSITION	67	Average Mark	67%
LITERATURE	90	Place on Class List	14ᵗʰ.
ELOCUTION	75	No. in Class	33
ENCH		**ACCOMPLISHMENTS**	Progress
TIN		PHYSICAL CULTURE & DEPORTMENT	*Poor.*
		GAMES	
STORY	56	PIANO	
		VIOLIN	
OGRAPHY	70	SINGING	
		DRAWING & PAINTING	
ASS DRAWING	55	NEEDLEWORK	*Very Good*

sses re-open on *Thursday 19ᵗʰ April 1928*

Signed *Sister M Loyola*

Parents are specially requested not to ask for interviews with the Head Mistress during School Hours.

The dining room, 1938. Part of the ground floor of St John's, which has subsequently been remodelled with partition walls and now houses the music department.

a distinction went to the front; those scoring a credit formed a semi-circle behind them; those who achieved passes formed a larger semi-circle around the outside, whilst the failures stood forlornly at the back. It must have been excruciating waiting to see whether you would be the last to be called, when you might receive stern admonition from the Sister Superior, and strong encouragement to do better. This practice continued into the 1960s.

In 1931 a small Sixth Form of six students was created, studying for matriculation exams for university entrance. Two years later Headmistress Sister Cécile introduced cookery, social sciences and Greek to the curriculum.

Pupils who attended the high school during the 1930s recalled that silence was kept on the stairs except during break, and that prefects ensured that the rule was enforced. The floors were immaculately polished by the maids, with the smell of polish being one forever associated with Notre Dame schooldays. It was regarded as a capital sin not to change your shoes when you went in to school, almost as bad as talking to boys!

The late Barbara Woodrow (née Woods), a pupil in the 1930s, provided a wonderful description of the uniform at that time:

> In September 1933 I was off to Notre Dame wearing the distinctive uniform of 'the convent girls'. In winter we wore navy velour hats, navy overcoats or gabardine mackintoshes, brown woollen stockings, and brown lace-up shoes (with brown strap shoes in school and brown plimsolls for sports). Instead of the traditional gymslips we wore navy pleated skirts with royal blue jumpers which, when pulled down, reached our knees. At the neck of our jumpers we wore a large blue bow with stripes for the colour of our house: Towneley in blue, Stafford in yellow, and Walsingham in green. In summer we wore navy blazers with 'ND' in gold on the top pocket, panama hats, and cotton dresses of a rather drab fawn colour covered with white spots encircled by black rings. We called them our frog-spawn frocks!

The girls of the high school were set in classes that followed one of two curriculum options – either they were in the Latin class (which also studied French and art) or in the French class (which took cookery and art). The vast majority of subjects were taught by the Sisters, although by this time there were a few 'civilian' or secular mistresses. Discipline in classes could be very strict, as witness this account from Barbara Woodrow:

Lord Mayor's visit for Prize Day, 1934. St John's Hall.

Sister Teresa Francis Snelgrove. Known to the pupils as 'Ambulo', Sister Teresa Francis served the school for forty-five years, teaching Latin, RE and Greek.

Sister Teresa Francis taught Latin and was always known amongst the pupils as Ambulo as that was the first verb she always taught [ambulo, 'I walk']. She was easily irritated and once, during our second year, we played a trick on her. Each girl, there were about thirty of us, had two marbles in the groove of our desks and when she walked into the classroom we all pushed our two marbles onto the floor. The floors were of polished wood and the noise was terrific. Ambulo stopped dead in her tracks, then swung round and walked out of the door, shutting it quietly behind her. A few moments later on our Form Mistress, Sister Carmela, came in and by the time she had finished telling us how despicable we were and how she was horrified at our behaviour we all felt terribly ashamed of ourselves. Our punishment was that for a whole week our lessons were to carry on in complete silence with instructions from the staff on the notice board. Homework was also increased. By the end of the week we were all very much chastened and each and every one made our apologies to Sister Teresa Francis.

Ambulo's name was Sister Teresa Francis Snelgrove and she was one of the great characters of Notre Dame. A fearsome disciplinarian, she taught Latin, RE and occasionally Greek at the school for over forty years. She was tender in religion and would weep over the Passion of Jesus, falling to her knees in the corridor amid the hustle of changing lessons when the Angelus bell rang

Class in St John's, 1935.

at noon, to recite the incarnation prayers and the three Hail Marys. She was to play a prominent role in limiting the damage to the school during the Second World War, clambering up a ladder to hose down the burning convent roof, and later kept bees at the hive under the school windows, donning a beekeeper's hat and veil to attend them.

By 1937 the school population had expanded to 460 pupils, and Spanish had been introduced as an alternative to French, along with classes in social sciences and citizenship, a progressive and enlightened policy.

The names of the recipients of the Cambridge school awards for 1937 provide a snapshot of the fashions of the era. There were two Joans, two Dorothys, two Bettys, two Kathleens and one each of Gladys, Barbara, Nancy, Monica, Myrtle, Daphne, Doris, Ruby and Margaret.

Surprisingly, the overwhelming majority of the children were not Catholic. Nevertheless they were expected to recite the Hail Mary between lessons, and also the series of Angelus prayers (celebrating the Annunciation and Incarnation) at midday. The few Catholic pupils had separate lessons on Divinity, and non-Catholics were only permitted to visit the chapel on special occasions provided the Sisters received written permission from their parents. At that time (and into the 1950s) children had the majority of their lessons in only one classroom and their teachers came to them, though there were separate classrooms for art, needlework, science and physical training (PT).

First Holy Communicants, 1938. Pupils in front of Lady Julian building are: Barry Conway (who later taught at the High School), Pat Norton, Mary Robinson, unknown, Ann Bender, Myra Brooks and Brian Kearney.

UNDER ATTACK: THE SECOND WORLD WAR

THE MOST DRAMATIC EVENTS IN THE HISTORY of the school occurred during the Second World War. From September 1939 to Easter 1944, Norwich considered itself in the front line. The city was classified as a 'neutral area' but no Norwich school was allowed to open after the summer holidays until it had adequate air-raid shelters. The dining room and cookery room in the high school (St John's) were approved for this purpose, both being partially below ground, along with the cloakroom of the boarding school (in the Lady Julian building). The necessary alterations were quickly made, and the school re-opened on 25 September 1939.

Norwich did not sustain serious damage from air raids until July 1940 when a raid killed thirty and injured a hundred in the city. The convent was not damaged at this time though bombs fell either side, in Surrey Street and Ber Street. Life in the convent was far from straightforward, vividly recalled in this account by the then Sister Superior Sister Cécile des Seraphims:

The convent and school had been almost miraculously preserved, but the strain on the Sisters was so great that sleeping accommodation was provided for them in the cellars [beneath the convent]. The very small cellar which houses the very big heating apparatus, and the adjacent still smaller cellar, a vegetable store-room, were converted into sleeping apartments for 30 people. Wooden shelves in the vegetable room were arranged as bunks, several basket chairs were brought in for the small of stature as well as Nursery School folding beds, and the rest of the community sat on camp stools wherever they could find available space. For several months these conditions endured for the larger part of almost every night.

During the latter part of 1940 and the beginning of 1941, Norwich, though not a primary target, shared in the major air-raids on Coventry, Birmingham, Merseyside and Manchester, for waves of German planes passed over the city on their way to the North and West, as well as to London. Occasionally bombs were dropped in the neighbourhood. During

Opposite: Norwich under attack, 29 April 1942. Looking up Rampant Horse Street, past the current premises of Marks and Spencer to St Stephen's church. Curl's Department Store opposite was completely destroyed. Debenhams now occupies this city centre site.

Preparatory school percussion band, 1938.

High school orchestra, 1938. Back row: Barbara Lee, Fay Ibison, Gwen Nicholson, Mary O'Meara, Agnes Mutimer, Eiluned Fish, Phyllis Taylor; middle row: Mercia Beech, Betty Ayton, Sheila Forman, Pat England, Sybil Blagden, Monica Kimberley, Monica Ayron; front row: unknown, Michael Regester, Bernadette Henderson, Daphne Cook.

the long hours of a raid the Sisters prayed, worked, read or slept according to inclination or opportunity, two remaining meanwhile on Warden duty, as well as the convent gardener, himself a warden, who patrolled the surrounding streets. Sometimes the sirens sounded four or five times during a single night, and this necessitated as many journeys from dormitories to cellar for those who preferred short spells in bed to

prolonged catacomb conditions. The same happened during the day, bringing the added anxiety for the safety of the children. During 'crash' warnings – betokening the dropping of bombs in the vicinity – the children prayed aloud, but in quiet periods lessons proceeded as usual in the shelters. At no time did the children show any signs of panic.

The damage from one of these passing raids trapped the Head Girl, Barbara Taylor, in the rubble of her home on Kett's Hill. Despite sustaining head injuries she guided rescuers to her location by singing. In later years she joined the staff of the school and became Head of English.

When the school re-opened in September numbers were down by about a hundred, as children had been evacuated to the countryside for safety. However, there were some new day pupils, for the school was now attended by a few refugees from Germany and Austria who had been placed with English families as part of the Kindertransport scheme, which helped Jewish children flee persecution in central Europe. Numbers in the boarding school had reduced to only twelve. The overall decline in numbers and the ending of the Order's teaching at Willow Lane Elementary School caused the Sisters considerable financial loss.

Following extensive damage to the city during raids in late April 1942, the older Sisters left the convent for safer areas in the country. The remaining Sisters moved to rural locations along the Dereham Road, in Salhouse and

Westwick Street, Norwich, 27 April 1942. Running from the ring road up to St Benedict's Street, factories along Westwick Street were destroyed by German firebombs during the Second World War. This picture shows the Wincarni's and Odol Works, sited close to where the Toys 'R' Us car park now stands.

at Costessey and travelled to school every day, some by bus, others in the luxury of a private car or the indignity of a closed meat cart or open lorry, which must have made a surreal sight. This brief episode did not last long, for the whole community returned to Surrey Street in June 1942.

On 26 June 1942 Norwich experienced another heavy air raid. Sister Cécile recorded the dramatic events:

> Three Sisters were acting as wardens, and when the Sisters in their cellar refuge were alarmed by a strong smell of burning, one of the three came down to say that all the windows on one side of the convent were out, and that the garden was covered with incendiary bombs, several of which had fallen on the convent roof. Immediately all the able-bodied Sisters, including the Superior, transformed themselves into fire-fighters, and by their united efforts saved the building from serious damage. Stirrup-pump teams got to work, and those bombs that had penetrated through the roof into the rooms below were quickly extinguished. Those which had lodged on the roof itself were more difficult to reach. However, several of the Sisters scaled ladders both inside and outside the house, to play the hose upon the fires, or to hack away portions of the burning rafters. All who were able took turns at the stirrup-pumps, while the others carried successive pails of water. Two devoted secular mistresses in fire-fighting kit rendered valuable service, as well as maids and gardeners, and eventually the four fires on the convent premises were brought under control. Meanwhile every window of the secondary school on the playground side had been shattered by high explosive bombs dropped on a church opposite, as well as those of the Preparatory School. Five incendiaries which fell on the school itself were dealt with by the Sisters on fire-duty there, but the ARP premises which adjoined the Preparatory School were a blazing inferno, and caused much anxiety. Both schools are some distance from the convent, and the Sisters went from the latter to combat this new danger, avoiding many incendiaries which were burning themselves out in the garden. Garden hoses and stirrup-pumps were played on the walls of the school, and on the bicycle shed, which was contiguous with the ARP premises, until the fire was got under control by the town authorities. Turning back to the convent the Sisters were horrified to see flames pouring

Preparatory school sack race, Costessey Hall, 1938. Taken in the grounds of the ruined hall, whose tower and parapets are visible in the background. The hall was the childhood home of Laura Stafford-Jerningham and the school had links with it until it fell into disrepair in the early twentieth century and was commandeered for troops during the First World War.

from the roof of the Boarding School above the head of the principal staircase. Two undiscovered incendiaries had made good progress there and it was necessary to call for the help of the Fire Brigade. Two firemen arrived, who, aided by four stirrup-pump teams, extinguished the fires, though a considerable portion of the roof had been destroyed. All danger was not over until 6am, and as it was impossible to have Mass that morning in the convent chapel, a priest from St John's came to give the Sisters Holy Communion. Later the Sisters cleared away the broken glass and debris – it was a Saturday so there was no school, and arrangements were made for the immediate repair of the damage which had not affected the main structure of the convent. By evening the Sisters could laugh over their adventures and mishaps, as when a hose was turned accidentally on to one of them, or another who begged a Sister 'to pump hard' as no water flowed, and then found that she had the leg of the stirrup and not the pump itself in the water.

One can only but admire the resilience and fortitude of the Sisters, and their efforts that helped save the school and convent buildings. School reopened, without boarders, in September 1942. The worst was over.

The boarding school premises (Lady Julian Building) were refurbished to accommodate 150 girls and boys in the preparatory school, newly organised on Montessori lines with lessons in singing, physical training and elocution. The former preparatory school building (St Joseph's) was used for cooking and domestic science. The first public prize evening took place in St Andrew's Hall in November 1947, with prizes presented by Leo Parker, the bishop of Northampton.

The Sisters' stoical attitude to adversity was readily apparent during the war years. As an example, on VE Day (Victory in Europe) Form 1 mistress Sister Teresa of the Trinity fell down the convent stairs. On her return to her class she observed 'Children, take it from me, when you are falling down the stairs there really isn't time for a good Act of Contrition.'

Stained-glass panel in Lady Julian Building.

Milk, 1949. From 1946 until 1971 milk was provided for schoolchildren above the age of seven. Here Jean Bunn, Vivienne Soman, and Betty Bealey enjoy their daily quota.

43

THE 1950S AND 1960S

BY THE END OF THE SECOND WORLD WAR, numbers in the high and preparatory schools had returned to pre-war levels, and the school continued to flourish.

Notre Dame followed the direct grant grammar school model, able to select students by ability following the eleven-plus exam. The majority of the girls came from families that paid termly fees but the school received a direct grant from the Ministry of Education in exchange for accepting a quarter of pupils on 'free' places. The high school remained exclusively for girls, although boys were admitted to the preparatory school. In 1951, along with all other schools in the country, Notre Dame introduced the General Certificate of Education Ordinary Level and Advanced Level exams ('O' and 'A' levels), examinations whose introduction initially caused some concern that they were designed only for the most able pupils.

However, the school did well in exams and also in public concerts, winning both the under-16 and whole school categories at the 1952 Norwich Festival of Music at St Andrew's Hall (out of eleven and four entries respectively).

The following year, 1953, began with several events to raise money for victims of the devastating North Sea floods of 31 January, when a hundred people were drowned in Norfolk alone. A happier occasion was celebrated in June to mark the coronation of Elizabeth II:

> At 1pm the school marched out onto the Green, led by the Head Girl, who bore the Standard. Formations were made and all sang 'Elizabeth of England'. After that the programme of dancing, skipping and apparatus work was begun. During an hour and a half items of interest and entertainment were produced. After 'God Save The Queen' the children withdrew to school for ice cream.

German, Russian and Italian were introduced into the curriculum and the

Opposite: Senior pilgrimage to Walsingham, 28 May 1952.

The Lady chapel during the Marian year, 1954. On the first floor of St John's, the Lady chapel is now used as a small teaching room.

May procession 1952. A composite shot giving an impression of the celebrations in honour of Our Lady.

The Blessing of the new Mary Bell, 21 November 1954. The bell was rung to mark the end of the Marian year on 8 December 1954.

school promoted the cultivation of marigolds, considered to be 'conducive to a good school spirit.' With their name derived from 'Mary's Gold', these flowers are associated with Our Lady, having being used as offerings to the Virgin by some of the earliest Christians. The annals record them as the school flower, though this has rather grown out of fashion. Saint Julie preferred the sunflower, extolling her Sisters to 'be like the sunflower that follows every movement of the sun, and keep your eyes always turned towards our good God'.

Pope Pius XII declared 1954 the first Marian year in the Church's history, with the purpose of increasing the faith of the people and their devotion to the Virgin Mother. In Norwich, the Sisters threw themselves wholeheartedly in support of the Marian year in honour of their namesake. Pilgrimages were organised for the First Years to Thetford; the Second Years to King's Lynn; the Third Years to London and the Fourth Years to Canterbury. In addition, over the Easter holidays groups of twenty-five to thirty-five girls went on pilgrimage to Lourdes, to Buckfast Abbey and to Walsingham. In June twenty children made their First Holy Communion in the convent chapel. The year was brought to a close by the ringing of the newly blessed Mary Bell at midday on 8 December.

The convent building remained strictly off-limits for children. Girls had to skirt past the convent when events were held on the Lady Julian Green. Children were extremely respectful to the Sisters, and stood still and bowed slightly every time a nun walked past, especially in the high school. For events such as assemblies the whole class or year would bow together in silence when a Sister entered the hall.

Numbers in the school continued to increase, so that by the mid-1950s there were over 600 pupils on site, the vast majority girls, but with boys accounting for up to a quarter of the approximately 200 preparatory school pupils. The increased number of children required more teachers, but because there was not an increase in the number of Sisters at the school, more and more positions went to lay staff, and the composition of the staff body quickly changed. In fact, the convent never consisted of more than thirty Sisters, and by this time most nuns were engaged solely in the invaluable services of running the house and chapel (as cook, laundress, sacristan etc).

The increase in the number of lay teachers had at least one unexpected consequence. Implementation of equal pay for women teachers, as stipulated

Below: Bus travel round London, 2 March 1954. After arriving by train at Liverpool Street Station forty-six Third Year pupils were taken by bus to visit shrines to Our Lady at Chingford, Muswell Hill, Willesden, Clapham, Cromwell Road and Warwick Street as part of the Marian year celebrations.

Below right: Pupils and staff continue to join the Eastertime pilgrimages with HCPT, the Pilgrimage Trust, to take children with disabilities to Lourdes for a week's break. This photograph shows Notre Dame pupils on pilgrimage in 1954.

Left: *Romeo and Juliet*, February 1954. In the 1950s and 1960s the school put on a series of highly acclaimed plays with excellent sets designed by the art department. Here Hilary Whiting is Juliet, and Sheila O'Donovan Romeo.

Below: *Romeo and Juliet* hand-painted programme, February 1954.

Romeo and Juliet, 1954. The wider cast. The Nurse was played by Linda Dennes, the Prince Rosemary Taylor, Friar Lawrence Valerie Carman, Old Capulet Valerie Cox, and Lady Capulet was played by Gretel Ives.

Above: Trip to the Midlands, July 1955. Thirty-three Second and Third Year pupils leave St John's to go on a week's tour of Midland industries and places of interest.

Above right: Boarding the bus to the Midlands, 1955. Form mistresses Miss Havran and Miss Upton accompanied the pupils on the trip.

by an amendment to the Burnham Report on national pay scales, meant that the school was facing a financial loss. Governors responded by increasing the fees from 9 guineas a term in September 1955 to 17 guineas a term the following year. Further increases inevitably followed. These resulted in a temporary dip in numbers, but this was eventually made up. As the high school was a direct grant girls' school, about a quarter of the places remained 'free' places, paid for by government funding.

Once enrolled at school pupils were divided into three ability streams – the most academic were in Form 1 Latin, next came an 'alpha' stream (the equivalent of the pre-war French group) and, for those of a more practical nature, the 'A' stream. Unfortunately the ritual of end-of-term 'semi-circles' continued for some time to come.

The school could accommodate a general increase in pupil numbers because it had acquired the land beyond the high school building. After a long battle during the mid-1950s, council plans to convert this site of the old Surrey Road Elementary Schools to a car park had been reversed. The

St Mary's, 1989. The former Surrey Road Elementary Schools, St Mary's eventually became the school canteen but was already past its prime.

area had for many years been used as a lorry park, but the brick wall separating it from the convent land was demolished and the vehicles disappeared. In July 1956 celebrations on Marigold Day marked the formal opening of four hard tennis courts on the site of the car park, and of the acquisition of a school building, which was renamed St Mary's. This Victorian building stood on what is now the lower playground, and was used as classrooms before becoming the school canteen.

Marriott Tennis Cup, 1957.

In spite of running a fee-paying selective school, the Sisters never forgot St Julie's admonition to exist 'only for the poor, absolutely only for the poor'. Every morning they used to provide a cup of tea and a bacon roll for down-and-outs from a shed on the green in front of the high school. On Christmas Day they even provided Christmas dinner!

Right through until the 1980s the site was never locked. Caretaker Roy Money can recall several occasions when the Sisters phoned during the early hours to request that tramps intent on sleeping off their inebriated state on the school's premises be politely removed to the local night shelter.

Caretaking staff were invited in to the convent once a year, at Christmas, for a glass of sherry and a mince pie, and a single carol round the Christmas tree. Staff did not venture up the convent drive and were not allowed in the car park area in front of the convent.

Form VI (Upper), July 1964. Back row: Elizabeth Eglington, Philippa Forbes, Lesley Wyles, Helen Podlesney; front row: Pat Embling, Carol Watling, Anne Futter, Lavinia Pointer, Pamela Gibson.

The school modestly celebrated its successes, and marked the centenary of its founding with a High Mass of Thanksgiving in the convent chapel in October 1964.

By 1966 there were 474 pupils, of which 193 were Catholic. Fees had increased to 87 pounds and 15 shillings a year, and almost a quarter of pupils benefited from 'free places'. The Sixth Form had expanded to fifty-nine pupils.

In 1968 Sister Joseph of the Holy Ghost completed her second five-year spell as head teacher, the first having commenced during the war years. Her successor was a thirty-seven-year-old Sister from Leeds who would steer the school through some of the greatest changes in its history during her twenty-eight years as head teacher.

SCHOOL IN TRANSITION:
SISTER MARY CLUDERAY

Sister Mary
Cluderay, 1993.

SISTER MARY CLUDERAY BECAME HEAD TEACHER on 1 September 1968. The only girl in a family of eight children she had attended Notre Dame High School in Leeds, and latterly had been head of RE at the Sisters' school in Battersea. Though she had been appointed under the name of Sister Peter Maria, shortly after becoming head teacher in Norwich she began to use her own name, Sister Mary. This apparently small step was perhaps indicative of her vision to make the community more outward-looking and inclusive, and to move it forward at a time of great change, both in the Church and in society.

Following the Second Vatican Council in the early 1960s, Sisters were permitted to wear a modified habit, followed by a transition to the dress of ordinary women, with only a Notre Dame cross for identification. The few

Some of the teaching staff, March 1971. Back row: Mrs Harvey (PE), Mrs Holme (maths), Mrs James (maths), Mr McDowell (physics and chemistry), Mrs Bradley (biology), Mrs Mullen (English), Mrs Holman (PE), Mrs Borrill (lab technician), Mrs Scotcher (geography); middle row: Mrs Howman (maths), unknown, Mrs White (maths), Miss Neal (science), Mrs Rawlence (Classics), Mrs Hadley (French), Miss Cocks (elocution), Sister Agnes McCready SND (religious education and general subjects), Mrs Baker (science); front row: Miss Trett (art), Miss Campling (French), Miss Francis (French), Sister Mary (head teacher and religious education), Miss Taylor (English), Miss Moulton (German), Miss Powell (history).

remaining teaching Sisters adopted these reforms to a varying degree, with the younger Sisters more receptive to change.

With the Labour government's promotion of a comprehensive system of free education available to all children, the Order decided to withdraw from fee-paying schools. The transition took some time, but the preparatory school (which had existed in Norwich since the turn of the century) closed in 1971, moving to the Dereham Road as a completely separate fee-paying school which still retains the Notre Dame name. The premises it vacated (which had earlier housed the boarding school) were renamed the Lady Julian building and were used for music, art and needlework. The Sisters' numbers had dropped over time and they vacated the dormitories on the

Bishop of the newly created Diocese of East Anglia Rt Rev Alan Clark blesses the statue of Our Lady of Walsingham during Mass in Lady Julian Hall, December 1976.

top floor. In 1976 these were converted to a Sixth Form common room, discreetly out of the way of the rest of the school.

The most significant change though was still to come. The government's phasing out of direct grant status meant that the school had either to become a comprehensive school, or exist separately as an independent. Becoming independent would mean that fees would need to be hugely increased and the school would become more exclusive. This was not in line with the original vision of the founding Sisters nor of an outward-looking Catholic church, so it was decided that the school would become comprehensive. As a comprehensive, not only would Notre Dame take pupils of all abilities, but teenage boys would enter the high school for the first time. The plans caused some anxiety among staff and parents, but nevertheless, driven by Sister Mary's conviction that this was the correct way to go, the decision was taken to proceed.

On 1 September 1979 Notre Dame opened as a voluntary aided co-educational comprehensive school; ownership passed from the Sisters of Notre Dame to the newly formed Diocese of East Anglia. Sister Mary

Boys, September 1979. High school boys first came to Notre Dame when the school converted from a direct grant girls' grammar school to a voluntary aided comprehensive. Here Sister Mary welcomes some of the new pupils on the first day of term.

welcomed the first seventy-two boys (out of 850 pupils), and at the same time welcomed the first male deputy head, Mr Lawrence Montagu. The next year the first eight boys entered the Sixth Form alongside 177 girls, and numbers of boys increased steadily until there were approximately equal numbers of girls and boys in the school. In spite of some initial difficulties, parental concerns regarding the admission of boys proved unfounded, and the transition to a comprehensive system went as smoothly as could be expected. CSE courses were introduced alongside GCE certificates to cater for all. The school continued its outward-looking perspective, with foreign language trips to Rouen, Bonn, Barcelona, Leningrad and Venice, but the school's sailing and equestrian teams were not to continue for much longer.

School choir at St Andrew's Hall, 1979.

The arrival of boys necessitated some expansion of the school's premises. The distribution depot on Finkelgate, formerly owned by tea and coffee merchants Lamberts, was acquired in 1979, re-named St Peter's and converted to woodwork, metalwork and technical drawing classrooms the following year. Eight science labs formed the top floor.

Initially the boys used the gymnasium at the new comprehensive in Hethersett and the playing fields at City College. In 1984 the school acquired and converted the bus station on Ber Street, removing underground diesel tanks, filling in inspection pits and levelling the floor to create the St Paul's Sports Hall, which allowed basketball, tennis, football, trampolining, table tennis and volleyball to flourish. However, space remained at a premium, and on more than one occasion a PE class was taken running up and down the stairs of nearby Bonds (now John Lewis), much to the bemusement of shoppers (and pupils!). The school still has no playing fields, and instead is grateful to the Hewett School for access to its playing fields.

The greatest threat to the school at this time was the proposal by Norfolk County Council to construct an inner ring road link in 1989, with the aim of easing traffic congestion. The favoured option, approved by councillors, was a £30 million route from Queen's Road (opposite Sainsbury's), across Surrey Street, between Norfolk Tower and Notre Dame and then under Ber Street via a tunnel emerging at Rouen Road. The

Llangollen Eisteddfod, 1982. Under Director Vyvyan Morris the choir was particularly successful, and took part in the national Eisteddfod.

planned route would have meant the loss of the main playground, and the demolition of St Mary's dining room, with the school site much reduced. Sister Mary, strongly supported by staff, pupils and an energetic Parent Teacher Association, led a vigorous and sustained campaign against the road link, both in the press and at County Hall. In 1994, following a public enquiry, the plans were finally dropped and the school was saved.

Sister Mary was a forward-thinking head teacher who managed the school's transition to a mixed, all-ability comprehensive, and insisted that the school retain its Sixth Form when there was a suggestion that it be closed. Like all the school's head teachers she was supported by a very able and committed staff who drove progress forward. Sister Mary put pupils at the heart of school life, and many of her reforms have stood the test of time. She introduced Open Week, an inclusive initiative that allows prospective parents to come and see the day-to-day activities of the school. She proposed that pupils elect the head students and that the Sixth Form uniform be abandoned, took a level-headed attitude to the teaching of sex and relationships education and was not afraid to tackle the issue of drugs which had emerged on schools' agendas nationwide. She took a lead on the teachers' boycott of Key Stage 3 exams and positioned the school for the twenty-first century. The convent finally closed in May 1994 but Sister Mary remained as head teacher and the last school Sister prior to her retirement at the end of 1996.

No Road, 1989. Council plans to construct a link road and tunnel between Queen's Road and Rouen Road would have meant the loss of the playground and the old St Mary's building. Sister Mary leads the pupils and staff in a memorable and ultimately effective protest.

No Road lobbying, 1989. Pupils protest outside County Hall.

STILL SERVING: NOTRE DAME TODAY

Sports day 2010.
The rejuvenation of
the House system
has reinvigorated
sports day, which
is now held at the
University of East
Anglia.

Sports day 2010.
The rejuvenation of
the House system
has reinvigorated
sports day, which
is now held at the
University of East
Anglia.

SOMEWHAT TO THE SURPRISE OF THE PRESS, the candidates shortlisted to succeed Sister Mary were all men. Charismatic Liverpudlian John Pinnington emerged successful, and became head teacher in January 1997. A deputy at the school for twelve years previously, he immediately altered the management structure by appointing a finance manager and a site manager, and strengthened the chaplaincy team.

In 2000 the school was successful in its bid to achieve language specialism status, and four years later added a second specialism, in science. Notre Dame was officially recognised as a Teacher Training School in 2003, echoing the original vision of the founders of the Order. Saint Julie would have approved.

Alongside these achievements, the great support of the Roman Catholic Diocese helped drive the transformation of the site. Governors, the school and the Diocese worked closely in partnership with Norfolk County Council to ensure the completion of an ambitious schedule of building projects. A new RE block and drama studio were created and the sports hall refurbished. The drama studio had occupied the chapel for a few years, and

Far left: John Pinnington and pupils, 1997.

Left: Bishop Michael Evans, Sister Mary and John Pinnington, 2004. The Diocese continues to be a very strong supporter of the school. Here Bishop Michael joins two head teachers to celebrate twenty-five years of the school becoming comprehensive, the re-dedication of the chapel and the extension and refurbishment of the St Paul's building.

Basketball success, 1999. The school's teams excelled, winning all leagues from under-13s to under-19s, a superb achievement.

Pupils in front of St John's, 2011.

59

Brian Conway, 2010.

once the studio moved to the St Paul's building the chapel was restored to its former glory, with the original pews returning from the cathedral. It remains central to the spiritual life and pastoral support of the school.

Equally significant was the successful bid for a £5 million new building to house the language department, library and canteen. A result of the combined efforts of the Diocese and the school (principally the bid writing skills of Gerry Aldus, Clerk to the Governors), in 2007 the new St Mary's building replaced its dilapidated Victorian namesake and provided bright, airy classrooms and modern canteen facilities. The most significant building project since 1926, it brought the school firmly into the twenty-first century. It allowed pupil numbers to increase to 1,400 (including a Sixth Form of almost 400), many of whom travel long distances to attend.

Further successful bids resulted in the creation of a science 'classroom of the future', and the fencing and surfacing of an all-weather play area where the tennis courts used to be. The school offered space for the Catholic Fund for Overseas Development (CAFOD) to run its East Anglia office and continued to support a wide range of charitable causes. Money was raised through a variety of initiatives, the largest being the whole school sponsored walk, still a highlight of the school year. The current route is a circuit round Whitlingham Broad.

Following John Pinnington's retirement in summer term 2010, deputy Brian Conway became only the third head teacher the school had had over the previous forty-two years. He further strengthened science facilities by adding two new laboratories to the St Peter's complex. In September 2011, building on the progress of previous years, the school achieved its first 'Outstanding' grading from Ofsted.

New signage was commissioned for the school buildings. The House system was regenerated with four Houses – Jerusalem, Rome, Santiago de

Defibrillator, 2009. Class 8JFA celebrate the school's acquisition of a defibrillator for use in emergency situations.

Left: Students prior to the Christmas celebration, 2012.

Left: School orchestra, 2009.

Below: Food hampers, 2010. The annual collection of food hampers and their distribution following the Christmas Carol celebration has become a Notre Dame tradition. Here class 9SCU proudly display their contribution prior to the end-of-term celebrations.

Above left: Papal visit to Great Britain, September 2010. Pupils from Notre Dame attended the papal address at St Mary's College Twickenham and the prayer vigil at Hyde Park during the Pope's visit. Here pupil Alex Dimminger greets Pope Benedict XVI as he stops to speak to young people from the Diocese on the steps outside Westminster Cathedral.

Above right: New school signage, 2013.

Opposite: St Mary's 2007. The new languages block was the result of collaboration between the school, the Diocese and the county council.

Compostela and Walsingham. Links with Catholic feeder schools were strengthened and formalised as a Catholic Cluster of schools.

On 1 March 2012 the status of Notre Dame changed again, when it became an academy, a publicly funded independent school. It is answerable directly to the Department for Education and to the Roman Catholic Diocese of East Anglia.

The school celebrates its 150th anniversary on 12 July 2014, Saint Julie's birthday. It continues to serve the Catholic population of Norfolk and north Suffolk, as well as the wider community. Generations of schoolchildren have passed through its doors. It seems well set to meet future challenges and looks forward with confidence to a bright future. Julie's maxim 'teach them what is necessary to equip them for life' continues to provide a lasting legacy. It is surely set to do so for some time to come.

HEAD TEACHERS OF NOTRE DAME HIGH SCHOOL SINCE 1930

1930	Sister Cécile des Seraphims
1933	Sister Mary Imelda
1943	Sister Joseph of the Holy Ghost
1947	Sister St James
1951	Sister Marie of the Presentation
1960	Sister Clare
1963	Sister Joseph of the Holy Ghost
1968	Sister Peter Maria (Mary Cluderay)
1997	Mr John Pinnington
2010	Mr Brian Conway

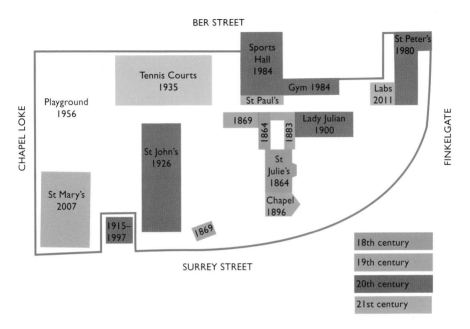

BER STREET

CHAPEL LOKE

FINKELGATE

SURREY STREET

Playground 1956

Tennis Courts 1935

Sports Hall 1984

St Peter's 1980

Gym 1984

Labs 2011

St Paul's

1869

1864

1883

Lady Julian 1900

St John's 1926

St Mary's 2007

1915–1997

1869

St Julie's 1864

Chapel 1896

18th century
19th century
20th century
21st century

Above: School buildings, showing dates of construction/acquisition. The oldest building is St Julie's and its adjoining stable block, which were built around 1760–70. Buildings are colour-coded according to the century they were constructed.

INDEX